The World *of* FESTIVALS

Philip Steele

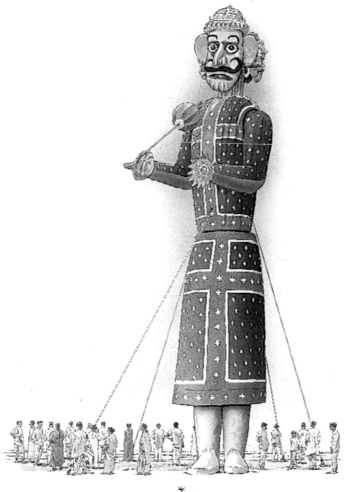

Macdonald Young Books

ACKNOWLEDGEMENTS

Illustrated by
Richard Berridge
Nicholas Hewetson
Stewart Lafford
Steve Noon
Roger Payne
Michael White
Neil Winstanley
Gerald Witcomb

Picture credits
6 C Bowman/Robert Harding; 7 ZEFA; 9 Hutchison; 10 Chris Bailey/Robert Harding
(top), Barros and Barros/Image Bank (bottom); 11 Robert Harding; 14 Hong Kong
Tourist Association (top), Robin Smith/Tony Stone Worldwide (bottom); 16 Mary Evans
(left), Alain Becker/Image Bank (right); 17 M Coyne/Image Bank; 18 Luca Inverizzi
Tetoni/Robert Harding; 19 Dr John MacKinnon/Bruce Coleman; 20 Bruce Coleman;
22 Adrian Evans/Hutchison; 23 Adina Tovy/Robert Harding; 24 British Film Institute;
25 Robert Harding (top), Eye Ubiquitous (bottom); 26 ZEFA; 27 Bruce Coleman; 28
Karen Benzian/Robert Harding; 29 Sammy Avinson/Robert Harding; 31 Robert Harding;
32-33 Tony Stone Worldwide; 35 Robert Francis/Robert Harding; 36 Ann and Bury
Peerless; 37 ZEFA; 38 Tony Stone Worldwide; 39 Robert Harding; 40 Robert Harding;
41 ZEFA

Edited by
Patience Coster

Designed by
Ian Winton and Steve Prosser

First published in 1996 by
Macdonald Young Books
61 Western Road
Hove
East Sussex BN3 1JD

Planned and produced by
Andromeda Oxford Limited
11-15 The Vineyard
Abingdon
Oxon OX14 3PX

ISBN 0-7500-1940-9
Printed in Singapore by KHL Printing

Contents

FESTIVALS AROUND THE WORLD

△ FASCHING MASK
Frightening wooden masks are worn during carnival, or Fasching, in southern Germany and Austria.

Flags flutter, bands play loud music, fireworks explode in the sky. There are feasts and street parties. People put on their best clothes or wear special costumes, fancy dress or masks. All over the world, people gather together to celebrate festivals, fairs, carnivals and holidays.

Although they may have their roots in ancient traditions, some festivals today are just for fun. Other festivals are more serious. They may mark the passing of the seasons, or be part of our religious beliefs. Some festivals recall great events of the past, or the lives of famous people.

ROMANS
About 1,800 years ago the Romans used to hold a winter festival called Saturnalia, in honour of their god Saturn. It was a time of feasting and fun. Whenever the Roman army won a great battle, there was a public holiday and a big parade.

SPANISH FERIA
Crowds pour into the city of Seville, in Spain, for the great spring fair, or Feria, normally held two weeks after Easter. Colourful banners decorate the streets and riders parade on horseback. The men wear broad-brimmed hats and the women wear beautiful, brilliantly coloured dresses of frills and lace.

EGYPTIANS
The ancient Egyptians worshipped about 2,000 different gods and most of them were honoured with their own festivals. Priests carried statues of gods from the temples in a public procession.

GREEKS
The ancient Greeks had all kinds of festivals to honour their gods. Some festivals were celebrated with plays. Others, like the first Olympic Games, were marked by sporting contests.

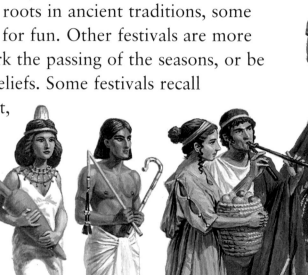

STREET CARNIVAL

Notting Hill Carnival is held each summer in London, England. It was started by people from the Caribbean who had settled in London, and is now one of Europe's biggest street festivals. Local people and school-children parade in spectacular costumes and dance to the music of steel bands.

INCAS
The Inca people lived in Peru about 600 years ago. Every year the emperor and all the nobles, dressed in gold and feather headdresses, went to the city of Cuzco. They held a great festival called Inti Raymi, in honour of the Sun god. People played pipes and drums. The festival is still celebrated today.

CELTS
The Celtic warrior shown here carries a long trumpet called a carnyx. The ancient Celts lived in central and western Europe and fought against the Greeks and Romans. They held four great festivals a year – Imbolc, Beltain, Lughnasa and Samhain. Celtic festivals included feasting, dancing and lighting bonfires. Sometimes humans were sacrificed to the gods.

INDEPENDENCE DAY USA
Independence Day is celebrated every year in the USA on 4 July. This American is taking part in a pageant, a festival in which people wear costumes to bring history back to life. His uniform dates back to 1776, the year in which the United States of America broke away from rule by Great Britain. The modern flag he is carrying is flown everywhere for July 4 celebrations.

BASTILLE DAY
On 14 July, people in France celebrate Bastille Day with flags and fireworks. This date marks the start of the French Revolution in 1789, when an angry crowd stormed the Bastille prison in Paris. France went on to become a republic (a country governed by an elected ruler, without a king or queen).

SPECTACULAR FIREWORKS
Fireworks are used to celebrate festivals and important public events all over the world. These beautiful rockets are bursting into the sky above Washington DC, the capital of the United States of America. They are marking Independence Day celebrations on 4 July. The first proper fireworks were made in China over a thousand years ago.

ELEPHANT PARADE SRI LANKA
A cannon shot marks the start of the Esala Perahera, a festival held by Buddhists in Sri Lanka at the time of the August full moon. Elephants are decorated with paint and their tusks are covered in jewels. They parade by night through the town of Kandy.

MARDI GRAS USA
In the American city of New Orleans, Mardi Gras is celebrated by marching bands playing jazz music. Mardi Gras or Shrove Tuesday is the last day before the period of Lent, when some Christians give up eating rich food.

MUMMERS
About 600 years ago in Europe, the Christmas holiday lasted for 12 whole days. People called mummers would dress up in strange clothes and animal skins, dancing and playing music. They would call from house to house, asking for money or food.

CARNIVAL IN BRAZIL
The week before Lent is the traditional time for carnival in many Roman Catholic countries. The carnival held in Rio de Janeiro, Brazil, is world famous. People parade through the streets in glittering costumes, doing a dance called the samba.

FAMILY FESTIVALS

△ GIRLS' DAY
Hina-Matsuri is a doll festival for girls, held in Japan on 3 March. Girls show their beautiful dolls to friends at parties.

Some of the first festivals we enjoy as children are held at home. Many of these are special days for members of the family. All over the world there are days for mothers, fathers, boys and girls, brothers and sisters. At these times we show how much we care for our relatives by giving presents and, in some countries, by holding private ceremonies.

Children's festivals often include toys, dolls or games. About 2,500 years ago in ancient Greece, young people used to give their toys and dolls as offerings to the gods, a sign that they had become teenagers and were leaving their childhood behind them. Many children's festivals have religious meanings. At the Izcalli festival, held in Mexico about 500 years ago, Aztec children went to the temple to have their ears pierced by a priest. The next day they would dance and feast in their homes in honour of the gods.

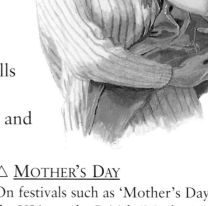

△ MOTHER'S DAY
On festivals such as 'Mother's Day' in the USA, or the British 'Mothering Sunday', children give flowers and cards to their mother, to thank her for her love and care. They may even make breakfast for her or bring her a cup of tea before she gets up in the morning!

◁ SAINT OF LIGHT
Lucia or Lucy is the Christian saint of light and brightness. She lived about 1,700 years ago. Her saint's day is 13 December. At this time of year, people in Sweden celebrate light and look forward to Christmas. Girls dress in white and wear headdresses of shining candles set in wreaths of evergreen leaves.

▷ FEAST OF THE KINGS

On Twelfth Night, the eve of 6 January, French Christians remember the three kings who visited Jesus. Families eat a cake containing charms. The child who gets a charm is crowned 'king' or 'queen'.

△ CARP KITES

On 5 May, a boys' festival is held in Japan. Kites in the shape of large fish called carp are made out of cloth or paper and hung outside every home. The carp represents the strength and courage the boys will need in their future lives.

RAKSHA BANDHAN

Raksha Bandhan is a Hindu festival for brothers and sisters, held in August. Sisters give their brothers a rakhi, a bracelet made of thread. This is tied around a charm which will bring good luck. In return, brothers promise to care for their sisters and look after them. Bracelets and rings are a sign of friendship. Many young people in western countries now make 'friendship bracelets' of plaited, coloured thread.

△ CHILDREN'S DAY IN TURKEY

Egemenlik Bayrami is a children's festival held each year in Turkey, on 23 April. It was started in 1920 by the man who founded modern Turkey, Mustafa Kemal Atatürk. Children perform folk dances in national costume, sing and play music, fly kites and watch puppet shows. They also eat sweet, sticky cakes.

PASSING THROUGH LIFE

△ WASHING AWAY SIN

This baby is being baptized. By placing her in water, the priest shows that she has become a Christian and a member of the Greek Orthodox Church.

All over the world, special events are held in honor of birthdays, growing up, getting married, and dying. These may be small family gatherings or occasions for large groups of friends or even whole villages to come together.

Presents are often given for birthdays. In China, an egg that is dyed red is given to a one-month-old baby because it symbolizes happiness. In parts of Africa, teenage girls and boys must paint their bodies or go through ceremonies to show that they are ready to become grown-ups. People everywhere wear their best clothes for weddings, giving gifts or holding feasts.

Funerals may be sad, but in some countries they are happy events, too. People celebrate the life that has come to an end or gather to wish the dead person well in the spirit world.

BAR MITZVAH

As Jewish children near their thirteenth birthdays, boys prepare for their Bar Mitzvah, and girls their Bat Mitzvah. At this ceremony, they take on the religious duties of an adult.

▽ BIRTHDAY CAKE

A girl blows out the candles on her birthday cake. She has been given presents and is having a party with friends. The song "Happy Birthday to You!" was written in the United States over 100 years ago and has even been sung by astronauts in space!

△ WEDDING CELEBRATIONS

When two people get married, they promise to love and care for each other. There are many different wedding ceremonies around the world. Generally people wear fine clothes to a wedding. In some countries, hundreds of people may come to the festivities, which may go on for several days!

◁ PIÑATA

These Mexican children are having a birthday party. They are blindfolded and given sticks to break the piñata. Inside it are candy or small gifts. All the guests scramble for them as they tumble to the ground.

DAY OF THE DEAD

During the Mexican Day of the Dead, a festival held on November 2, people visit their family graves. They leave flowers and candles there and eat a kind of sweet bread, leaving some behind as an offering to the dead. They give each other sweets in the shape of skulls.

MAKE YOUR OWN PIÑATA

Have a party, Mexican-style! You can make your piñata with papier-mâché.

You will need: 2 balloons, old newspapers, wall-paper paste (or flour-and-water paste), a brush, a pin, a knife, paints, string—and some candy.

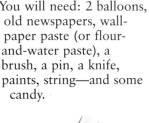

1. Start making the piñata one week before your party. Blow up two balloons, one large and one small. Tear up the sheets of newspaper into small pieces. Dip the pieces in the paste and layer them over both balloons. Let them dry overnight.

2. When both balloons are dry and rigid, use paper and paste to join them together. The small balloon can be the animal's head, the large

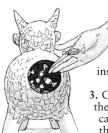

balloon its body. Build legs and horns with paper and paste (empty paper rolls will also work). Wait for them to dry. Now pierce the larger paper-covered balloon with the pin, until the balloon inside bursts.

3. Cut open the back of the piñata and fill it with candy. Then cover up the hole with new paper and paste. When this too has dried, you can paint the whole animal in bright colors. On the day of your party, hang it out of reach. Give your guests sticks and let the fun begin!

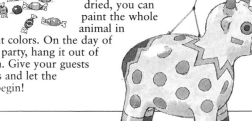

▽ HINDU FUNERAL

Funerals on the island of Bali, in Indonesia, are festivals which involve everybody in the village. The islanders follow the Hindu religion and they burn, or cremate, the dead. The villagers build a tower made of bamboo. They also make a large model of a black or white bull or a red lion. After a grand procession, the body is placed in the model on the tower and set on fire. The ashes are later scattered in a river or the sea. Hindus believe the soul never dies and that people are reborn to live a new life.

▷ CANADA DAY

National Day in **Canada** is 1 July. On this date in 1867 the various parts of Canada, which had formerly been ruled by the British, became a united country. This new Dominion of Canada had its own government for the first time.

△ US INDEPENDENCE DAY

National Day in the **United States of America** is Independence Day on 4 July. The United States' flag, the 'Stars and Stripes', is flown from buildings, and people hold parties. Marching bands parade through the streets.

▷ ST DAVID'S DAY, WALES

On 1 March, people in **Wales** wear national emblems, such as a daffodil or leek. They sing and play the harp at concerts. St David, the patron saint of Wales, lived 1,400 years ago.

▷ NATIONAL DAY, NETHERLANDS

On 30 April, the **Netherlands** National Day, people honour their queen. The official colour of the Dutch royal family is orange, so some children paint their faces orange! There are many fairs, and musicians play at street markets.

△ MEXICAN INDEPENDENCE DAY

In **Mexico**, National Day is 16 September. People gather in the centre of Mexico City. The president calls out for freedom and rings a bell. This is what happened in 1810, when Mexico rebelled against Spanish rule and became an independent country.

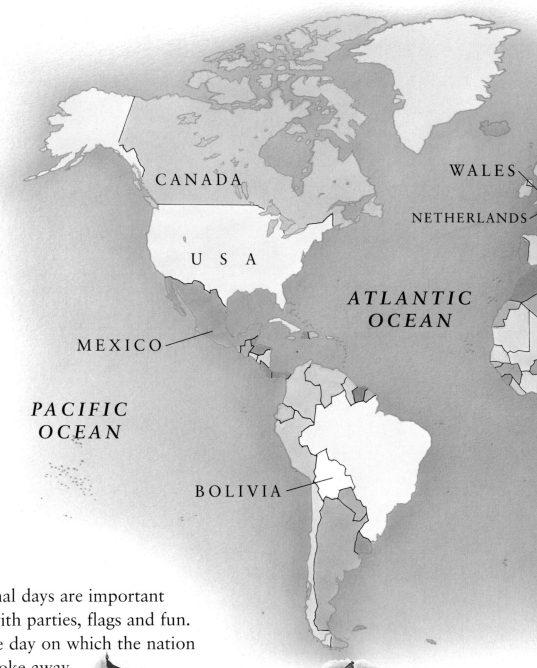

CANADA

U S A

WALES

NETHERLANDS

ATLANTIC OCEAN

MEXICO

PACIFIC OCEAN

BOLIVIA

NATIONAL DAYS

Throughout the world, national days are important holidays that are celebrated with parties, flags and fun. These festivities may mark the day on which the nation was first set up, or when it broke away from foreign rule. They may recall a famous battle or revolution, or the birthday of a king or queen. In some Christian countries, the day honours a 'patron saint', a holy person specially linked with that nation.

◁ NATIONAL DAY, BOLIVIA

The South American country of **Bolivia** takes its name from the soldier Simón Bolívar, who in 1825 freed the land from 300 years of Spanish rule. Bolivian National Day is celebrated with flags and parades, on 6 August.

◁ REPUBLIC DAY, ITALY

Before 1871, **Italy** was made up of many small countries. A man called Giuseppe Garibaldi helped to unite the country under a king. 2 June now celebrates the day in 1946 when Italy became a republic.

▷ GREEK INDEPENDENCE DAY
In **Greece**, the National Day is 25 March. It dates back to the year 1924, when the country first became a republic. There are many parades in national costume and festivals of folk dance and music.

▷ NATIONAL DAY, RUSSIA
In **Russia**, 7 November is a public holiday that recalls the Revolution of 1917. Russia now has two National Days, as Independence Day, 12 June, marks the collapse of the Soviet Union in 1991.

▷ INDIAN NATIONAL DAY
Elephants lead soldiers and marching bands in splendid uniforms through the streets of Delhi. This city is the capital of **India**, whose National Day is on 26 January. This marks the day in 1950 when India became a republic.

▽ NATIONAL DAY, JAPAN
National Day, or National Accession Day, in **Japan** takes place on 11 February. The nation honours Jimmu, who is said to have been the very first emperor of Japan. Legends say that he came to the throne in 660 BC.

▽ NATIONAL DAY, INDONESIA
The tropical islands of **Indonesia** have many festivals of dance and of horseriding skills. Their National Day is celebrated on 17 August, the date in 1945 when the country became free from rule by Japan.

▽ WAITANGI DAY
New Zealand's National Day, Waitangi Day, is on 6 February. It commemorates the day in 1840 that the islands' Maori people agreed to British rule. Soon after this, wars broke out between Maoris and European settlers.

ITALY
GREECE
RUSSIA
JAPAN
INDIA
TANZANIA
INDONESIA
AUSTRALIA
NEW ZEALAND

◁ NATIONAL DAY, TANZANIA
In **Tanzania**, 9 December is the National Day. On this date in 1961 the country became independent from British rule. On the same day one year later, Tanzania became a republic under the leadership of its first prime minister, Julius Nyerere.

◁ AUSTRALIA DAY
British prisoners were not very happy when they arrived in **Australia** on 26 January 1788 – they had to build a new colony! But this date marked the start of the modern nation, and is now honoured as Australia Day. This public holiday falls during the hot Australian summer.

REMEMBERING THE PAST

Festivals held in memory of a famous person or an important event are called commemorations. They are usually held on the same day each year, and may honor, for example, a famous poet, a great explorer, a significant battle, or a king or queen. People hold parties and celebrations and fireworks displays.

HONG KONG BUN FESTIVAL

A festival is held each May on the island of Cheung Chau, near Hong Kong, to commemorate the end of a plague that occurred long ago. Children are carried through the streets on poles, and lucky buns are piled on high towers.

△ BURNS NIGHT

On Burns Night, January 25, people of Scottish descent celebrate the birth in 1759 of Robert Burns, Scotland's greatest poet. The bagpipes are played as a haggis (a dish of meat and oatmeal) is carried into the feast.

Crowds also gather to honor the memory of people who have died in disasters or war. At these events there is often a moment of silence, when people stop to think about those who have died. In Great Britain, Remembrance Day, held on November 11, marks the end of World War I, in which millions of young soldiers were killed in battle.

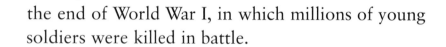

◁ THANKSGIVING

In 1621, a group of English settlers in North America gave thanks to God for the first harvest in their new home. Today, American families celebrate Thanksgiving with a turkey dinner on the fourth Thursday of November.

ANZAC DAY

On Anzac Day, April 25, Australia's armed forces parade in front of the National War Memorial in Canberra, the capital city. Each year Australians and New Zealanders remember a tragic battle that took place during World War I. On April 25, 1915, troops of the Australia and New Zealand Army Corps (ANZAC) landed on the coastline of Turkey, near Gallipoli. In the following months, 11,000 of them were killed, along with many young French and British soldiers.

▷ KINGS AND QUEENS

Queen Elizabeth II of Great Britain reviews her troops on horseback on the second Sunday of June every year. This 200-year-old ceremony, called 'Trooping the Colour', is part of her official birthday celebration.

◁ JOAN OF ARC

Joan of Arc, the French girl-soldier, is honoured on 30 May, the day she was burnt to death by the English in 1431. She was made a Christian saint in 1920.

▷ GEORGE WASHINGTON

George Washington, the first president of the USA, was born in Virginia on 22 February 1732. His birthday, now celebrated on the third Monday of each February, is a public holiday all over the country.

△ BONFIRE NIGHT

'Remember, remember the fifth of November – Gunpowder, Treason and Plot.' This old rhyme reminds British children of the date in 1605 when a man called Guy Fawkes tried to blow up the King and parliament with gunpowder. He failed, and was hanged for treason. Every year children collect money to make a 'guy' – a model of Guy Fawkes made from stuffed clothes and a mask. The guy is burnt on a big bonfire. People hold firework parties and eat baked potatoes and treacle toffee.

◁ MARTIN LUTHER KING

In the USA, Martin Luther King is honoured on 15 or 16 January. This great African American campaigned for justice and civil rights. He was killed by a gunman in 1968.

ONE SPECIAL DAY

Most festivals are held over and over again, once a year or perhaps just once every ten years. But some festivals take place only once. They may commemorate an anniversary, such as 500 years since the founding of a particular city, or some great event in history. Spectacular ceremonies may be held at the coronation of a king or a queen or when someone becomes president. Special postage stamps are often issued to commemorate these events that fall outside the normal calendar of festivals.

A new century is always marked by public celebrations. And the start of a new millennium, as in the year 2000, deserves a very special festival indeed.

A NEW GERMANY

On 3 October 1990, Germany became a united country again. Since 1949 it had been divided into two separate nations, the German Democratic Republic and the Federal Republic of Germany. Crowds gathered to celebrate in the centre of Berlin.

△ COLUMBUS DAY

In 1992 many countries celebrated the 500th anniversary of the date when explorer Christopher Columbus first landed in the Americas.

▷ AFRICAN CORONATION

Throughout the world, royal births, coronations, weddings or funerals are marked by glittering processions, splendid religious ceremonies and vast public gatherings. At his coronation, the ruler of Ghana's Asante people appears before his people wearing priceless gold ornaments and shaded by a ceremonial umbrella.

▷ VE Day

On 8 May 1995, people in the United Kingdom and many other European countries celebrated the fiftieth anniversary of peace coming to Europe, at the end of the Second World War. This special VE ('Victory in Europe') day was marked by street parties, dancing and the lighting of beacons. Many people wore 1940s dress.

Australian Bicentennial

Aboriginal people have lived in Australia for tens of thousands of years, but in 1788 the first Europeans settled on the continent. The 200th anniversary of that date was celebrated on 26 January 1988. The skyline of Sydney was lit up by fireworks and thousands of boats sailed into Sydney Harbour to join in the fun. Parties, concerts and sporting events were held to remind people of this important date.

▽ Independence Celebrations

Thousands of balloons rise into the air, coloured red, white and blue – the colours of the US flag. In the United States, every 4 July is a fun-filled holiday. But in 1976 the celebrations were unforgettable. They marked a milestone in American history – the 'bicentennial', or 200th anniversary of independence from British rule.

CHANGE AND RENEWAL

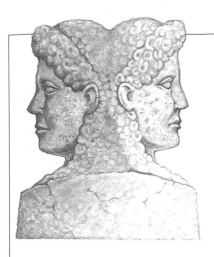

In ancient times in northern climates it was very hard to survive through the cold, dark months of winter. Nobody could grow crops in the frozen earth. There was little food and people often went hungry.

Many people used to believe that the Sun was a god. They prayed that he would defeat the spirits of darkness and bring back the warm sunshine of spring. They held dances and festivals to scare away evil spirits and to welcome the return of the Sun. Even when people turned to other gods and religions which came to replace the Sun god, they still held special festivals to mark New Year and spring.

Today we still look on the New Year as a time of hope and change, when we make plans for the future. In Scotland, New Year's Eve ('Hogmanay') is marked by parties and traditional dancing. In the Netherlands there are bonfires in the streets and elaborate firework displays. In India, the first day of the Hindu year is a day of feasting. It is believed to be a lucky day to start any new venture. Throughout the world, in both cold and warm climates, New Year is a time of celebration, with dancing, music and processions.

△ JANUS

The first month of the year, January, takes its name from Janus, the Roman god of beginnings and endings. Statues show him with two faces. One looks back to the past. The other looks forward to the future.

▷ CHINESE DRAGON

A beautiful paper dragon is carried through the streets to mark the Chinese New Year, or 'Spring Festival'. Firecrackers explode to frighten away evil spirits. Because the date of the Chinese New Year depends on the phases of the moon, it can take place between 21 January and 20 February. This is the most important holiday of the year in China. Doors are decorated with New Year greetings. Families get together for feasts and give each other presents.

BURMESE NEW YEAR

Water is splashed and sprayed around by happy crowds in Myanmar (Burma) to mark their New Year. The festival is great fun, but it has a serious side for the participants, who are Buddhists. At this time of year they pour water on their heads. This shows that they are 'washing away' the old year and making themselves clean and pure for the coming months.

PEACH BLOSSOM AT TET

A crowd in northern Vietnam walks through the fields carrying branches of peach blossom, a sign of renewal and hope for the future. They are celebrating the festival of Tet, the Vietnamese New Year. The festival lasts for three days.

▽ MAY DAY

May Day (1 May) has always been the date when northern Europeans welcomed spring. In the Middle Ages, people wore green leaves in their hats and danced outdoors. Today, many old May Day customs remain. These English children in medieval dress are dancing around a 'maypole', causing the ribbons to be twisted round the pole.

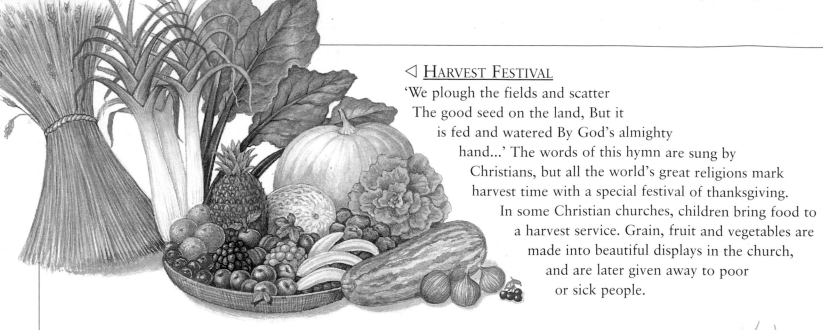

◁ HARVEST FESTIVAL
'We plough the fields and scatter
The good seed on the land, But it
is fed and watered By God's almighty
hand...' The words of this hymn are sung by
Christians, but all the world's great religions mark
harvest time with a special festival of thanksgiving.
In some Christian churches, children bring food to
a harvest service. Grain, fruit and vegetables are
made into beautiful displays in the church,
and are later given away to poor
or sick people.

SEASONAL FESTIVALS

Midsummer, autumn and the dark days of winter have their own celebrations. Many of these date back thousands of years and include dancing, music, bonfires and processions. Festivals around the world mark the sowing of seed, the coming of the rains and the harvest. Some of the first religious festivals were held in Stone Age times, at the start of the hunting season. Hunters would dress up in the skins and horns of animals and perform magical dances to bring good luck. Today, in countries from eastern Asia to western Europe, fishermen ask priests to bless their boats and nets each season.

SWEDISH MIDSUMMER

Fiddle and accordion music welcomes in a hot Midsummer's Day in the Swedish countryside. Folk dancers in traditional costume form a circle outside the church. Many of Europe's seasonal festivals, like this one, date back long before the days of Christianity.

◁ KWANZAA

Most harvest festivals are very ancient. Kwanzaa is a very new one. This seven-day December festival was started in the 1960s by African-Americans in the USA. Kwanzaa (meaning 'first fruits') celebrates the year's harvest in Africa. Fruit, vegetables and corn cobs are placed on a special mat. This is a time for the African-American family to learn about the traditions of their African ancestors and about their languages and ways of life. Seven candles, black, green and red, are lit during the Kwanzaa festival.

MAKE A CORN DOLLY

At harvest time people used to make models from the last sheaf of wheat or corn to be cut. Some people still make them for harvest festival. Corn dollies made from wheat come in all different shapes; but this one made from corn husks is doll-shaped.

You will need: the leaves or husks from about 8 fresh corn cobs, cotton wool, some string or tough thread and a pair of scissors.

1. To make the head and body, take a couple of corn husks and overlap them lengthways. Place a sausage-shaped roll of cotton wool in the hollow of the husks, bend the husks over and tie them firmly at the neck and waist. Slide a rolled husk, with the ends tied for hands, through the body.

2. Position the arms midway between the doll's neck and her waist. If the cotton wool stuffing spills out through the armholes, push it back inside the body.

◁ FISHING AT ARGUNGU

A spectacular two-day festival marks the start of the fishing season each February at Argungu, in northern Nigeria. Thousands of men and boys wade into the Sokoto River, carrying nets and big gourds called calabashes. They drive large fish called Nile perch, some of them weighing up to 70 kilograms, into the shallow water where they can be caught. There are displays of 'kbaci' (bare-hand fishing), swimming and canoe racing. Excited crowds line the river banks.

3. To make the skirt, place some husks around the figure's waist so that they cover her head and body, and tie them firmly in place at the waist. Now fold the top ends down to make a skirt and trim them straight across the bottom.

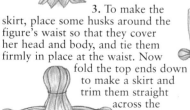

4. Stand your corn dolly upright on her skirt and keep her through the winter until the following spring, when the new crops start to grow.

WORLD GATHERINGS

World gatherings include great sporting events such as the football World Cup or the Olympic Games, world fairs or 'expos', and international trade fairs. Some pop music festivals are huge, too: almost a third of the world's population watched the televised 'Live Aid' concerts of 1985, which raised money to help victims of a terrible famine in Africa.

Surprisingly, many of these modern gatherings have ancient origins. The Olympic Games started in ancient Greece. We know the games were being held in 776 BC, and even then they may already have been celebrated for 600 years. They were started up again in 1896. Great fairs and markets, the forerunners of world 'expos', were held in Europe during the Middle Ages at trading centres such as Nuremberg in Germany. Air travel has now made it possible for people from all over the world to travel to big festivals; and satellites in space have allowed billions more to watch events live on television.

△ OLYMPIC FLAME
The Olympic Games started as a religious festival. The sacred flame is still carried from the site of one Olympics to the next, and burns throughout the games.

◁ WORLD 'EXPOS'
Expo '92 was billed as 'the event of the century'. It was held in the Spanish city of Seville in 1992 and marked the 500th anniversary of Columbus' voyage to the Americas. Over a hundred countries built special pavilions and exhibition halls on the site. They displayed the wonders of modern technology and architecture, and hosted art exhibitions, concerts and displays of dancing. Visitors came from all over the world.

◁ STADIUM OF WORLD SPORT

The ancient Olympic Games celebrated athletic skills such as running, jumping, discus- and javelin-throwing. They were also festivals of peace. Greek states were not allowed to take part if they were at war. The modern games celebrate international understanding as well as sport. Athletes from over 170 nations may take part. They parade around the stadium as the games are opened.

COLOUR AND SPECTACLE

A dazzling display of colour opened the 25th Olympic Games of modern times, in 1992. These were held in Barcelona, the capital of Catalonia in Spain. Over 10,000 athletes took part in 26 different sports. The 1996 games are being held in Atlanta, in the American state of Georgia.

▷ WINTER OLYMPICS

The Winter Olympic Games are a world gathering for winter sports champions from 60 or more nations. Like the main Olympics, they are held every four years. Events include bobsleigh and luge, skiing, skating and ice hockey.

◁ WORLD CUP

One of the greatest international sporting festivals is the association football (soccer) World Cup. The modern game of football was first played in the 19th century by the English (seen here winning the World Cup in 1966). The World Cup is held in a different country every four years – in 1994 it was the turn of the USA.

CELEBRATING THE ARTS

Dance, music and drama were an important part of the very first festivals. They were ways of honouring the gods. The first drama festivals grew out of religious festivals held in ancient Greece. Competitions were held for the best plays. In Wales (Great Britain) today, poets, writers, musicians and singers all compete with each other at festivals called 'eisteddfodau'.

All kinds of art play an important part in our lives. Special festivals are held to celebrate sculpture, painting, crafts, poetry, folk dance and ballet and every kind of music from classical to jazz, from country to rock and 'techno'. Arts festivals may feature the work of a particular artist or group of artists. They may aim to bring artists together from different parts of the world. And the mood of fun and celebration spreads far beyond the concert halls, theatres and galleries. On the 'fringe' of an arts festival there are often other unofficial performances, with acting, music or dancing in the streets.

△ LIGHTS, CAMERA, ACTION!

A poster advertises a film festival in London, England. Film festivals give people a chance to see the latest releases. Some festivals give prizes.

▽ JOINING OF HANDS

An Inter-Celtic festival is held in Brittany each year to celebrate the culture of the Celtic peoples of modern Europe – the Bretons, Galicians, Cornish, Welsh, Manx, Irish and Scots. It includes folk dancing and music, bagpipe playing, arts and crafts, and sports. All the Celtic regions are famous for their festivals, which have helped to keep alive many traditional art forms.

▽ All the World's a Stage

A performance of *Henry IV*, by the English playwright William Shakespeare (1564-1616), casts its magic over the audience at an open-air drama festival. Famous festivals of theatre are held all over the world, from Stratford, Ontario, in Canada, to Epidauros in Greece. It is in the religious festivals of ancient Greece that European theatre has its origins.

The Edinburgh Festival

A military festival, with parades and marching bands, is called a tattoo. The Edinburgh Tattoo is held each August in the capital city of Scotland. Pipers play in the old castle, high above the city. Meanwhile the streets below are taken over by one of the world's largest and most exciting international arts festivals. The Edinburgh Festival celebrates theatre, classical music, dance, film, television, poetry and even circus.

Pacific Arts Festival

Feasts and festivals have always been popular with the Melanesian, Micronesian and Polynesian peoples who live on the thousands of small islands in the Pacific Ocean. And no Pacific celebration is complete without singers and dancers dressed in garlands of flowers. This 1988 Pacific Arts Festival was held on the island of Tahiti.

△ Celebrating Jazz

Jazz music was born in the United States of America about 100 years ago, and was invented by African-Americans. It is now hugely popular. Famous American jazz festivals were first held in New Orleans, Louisiana and in Newport, Rhode Island. Today, many cities around the world hold their own jazz festivals.

Fun Festivals

We don't always need a special reason to enjoy ourselves. Many festivals have no other purpose than making merry. Some of them started as religious or historical festivals, but the reason for holding them has been long forgotten. Carnival was originally the last chance to feast before Lent, the Christian period of fasting and prayer. But today, carnival is just a festival of fun.

Halloween is a scary fun festival, held on 31 October. It dates back through the Christian festival of All Hallows' or All Saints' Eve to the ancient Celtic festival of Samhain, when people thought that the spirits of the dead could be seen. The Celts were originally head hunters who hung the heads of their enemies in their huts. At Halloween we still decorate our houses with heads made of pumpkins or turnips. Many festivals have no ancient history. They are simply a chance for people in a village or town to hold a fête or a summer fair, with coconut shies, fancy dress competitions, music and sports.

△ PUMPKIN HEAD
At Halloween, pumpkins are hollowed out and carved with eyes and mouths. A candle is placed inside the 'head' to make it glow.

△ PALIO
Horse riders race through the streets of Siena, Italy, during the Palio.

△ PANCAKE DAY
On Shrove Tuesday in England there are races in which people toss pancakes.

CARNIVAL IN RIO

The carnival in Rio de Janeiro, Brazil, is one of the most famous in the world. In the old days it was just a chance for fooling around. People threw flour, sand and perfumed water at each other. But it turned into a four-day festival of the dance called the samba. Tens of thousands of people in costume dance through the streets.

△ NOTTING HILL
Glittering costumes are worn at the carnival in London's Notting Hill.

△ MARDI GRAS
Marching bands play jazz during Mardi Gras in the city of New Orleans.

△ FASTNACHT
Ribbons and masks are worn on Fastnacht in Lindau, Germany.

△ MALMÉDY
Huge top hats on parade for carnival in the town of Malmédy, Belgium.

△ TRINIDAD
Trinidad has the most spectacular carnival parades in the Caribbean.

▽ TRICK OR TREAT
The Halloween festival, which started in parts of the British Isles, has become particularly popular in the USA. Children put on masks and dress up as witches or ghosts. They knock on the doors of houses in their neighbourhood, and say they will play a trick on people if they are not given a 'treat', such as sweets.

MAKE A HALLOWEEN MASK

Although you can buy masks for Halloween, it is much more fun to make your own. You might want to look like a devil, a witch, a ghost, a skeleton, a werewolf or a goblin.

You will need: a sheet of stiff card, scissors, a pencil, paints and a brush, sticky tape, a short length of stick, any old scraps such as fur or wool.

1. Draw the outline of the mask on a sheet of card, measuring it for size against your face. Draw eye-holes and a hole for the mouth. Cut it out.

2. Paint the mask with creepy designs and colours. When it is dry you might want to stick on furry or woolly beards or eyebrows.

3. Use sticky tape to bind the back of the mask to the short stick. Put on your costume – and off you go to haunt the neighbourhood. Just one word of warning – tell your parents where you are going and what you are doing.

MOOMBA

The Moomba festival takes place each year in Melbourne, Australia. It lasts for a week after Labour Day, in early March. Its aim is simple – getting together and having fun. There are boat races on the Yarra River, parades, and art shows.

JEWISH FESTIVALS

Nearly 18 million people around the world follow the Jewish religion, which is called Judaism. They believe there is only one God, that the son of God has not yet descended from Heaven, and that the Jewish people have been specially chosen to bring God's word to the world. In Israel, the ancient homeland of the Jewish people, eight out of ten people believe in Judaism. Two of the most important and solemn Jewish festivals are Rosh Hashanah (the Jewish New Year) and Yom Kippur, when people pray to be forgiven for their sins.

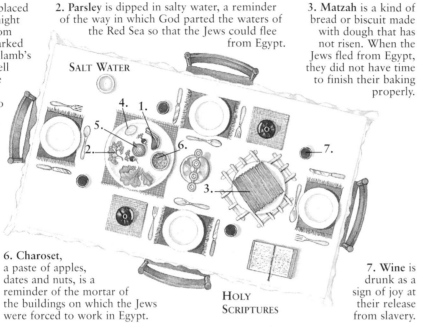

1. A lamb bone is placed on the table. The night before they fled from Egypt, the Jews marked their porches with lamb's blood. Scriptures tell how that night, the angel of death brought a plague to the Egyptians, but 'passed over' the Jewish houses.

4. An egg is a symbol of spring, of new life and hope.

5. Bitter herbs, onions or horseradish make tears come to the eyes, recalling the suffering of the slaves.

2. Parsley is dipped in salty water, a reminder of the way in which God parted the waters of the Red Sea so that the Jews could flee from Egypt.

SALT WATER

6. Charoset, a paste of apples, dates and nuts, is a reminder of the mortar of the buildings on which the Jews were forced to work in Egypt.

HOLY SCRIPTURES

3. Matzah is a kind of bread or biscuit made with dough that has not risen. When the Jews fled from Egypt, they did not have time to finish their baking properly.

7. Wine is drunk as a sign of joy at their release from slavery.

BRINGING OF LIGHT

The festival of Hanukkah is held in December. On each day of the festival a new candle is lit on the menorah, a nine-branched candlestick.

△ PASSOVER

Passover, or Pesach, is held in spring. A meal called Seder takes place on the first night of Passover. Here Jewish people eat special kinds of food, which reminds them of their history. Thousands of years ago, they were released from slavery in Egypt by the prophet Moses.

▷ SUCCOT

After fleeing Egypt, the Jewish people spent many years wandering in the desert, searching for lands they could settle. In the autumn festival of Succot, little shacks ('succot') made of branches and leaves are put up outdoors, to remind Jews of the tents they lived in after their flight from captivity.

◁ THE TORAH
The Jewish Holy Scriptures are called the Torah. The scriptures describe how God gave the Law, telling people how to live a good life, to the prophet Moses. The feast of Shavuot, or Pentecost, honours this event.

YOM KIPPUR
The blowing of the 'shofar', or ram's horn trumpet, marks the end of Yom Kippur, or 'Day of Atonement'. Yom Kippur ends a period called 'The Ten Days of Repentance', a time each year when Jewish people remember the things they have done wrong, and promise to do better the following year.

◁ PURIM
Children enjoy fancy-dress parades, carnivals and noisy parties at Purim. This festival of springtime fun, held in February or March, reminds children how, long ago, a wicked man called Haman plotted against Jewish people living in Persia. They were saved by Queen Esther, the Jewish wife of the Persian king. When the ancient story is read out at Purim, everybody boos the evil Haman!

▷ CRADLE OF THE JEWISH FAITH
The Jewish people escaped from slavery in Egypt about 3,200 years ago. They settled in the land of Israel, but over the ages many were scattered by wars and invasions. About 100 years ago, Jews began to return to live in the region shown on this map. They founded the state of Israel in 1948.

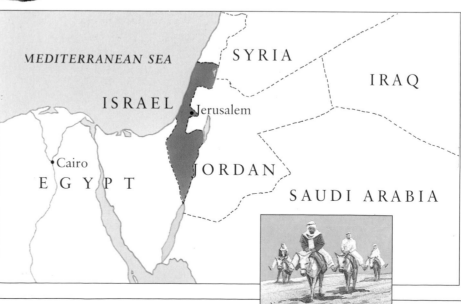

CHRISTIAN FESTIVALS

△ EASTER EGGS
The Easter festival marks the day when Jesus rose from the dead. Eggs are symbols of new life. Patterned eggs are traditional in Ukraine, and Russian Easter eggs were once made of silver and set with jewels! Most Easter eggs today are made of chocolate.

Christianity shares many of its beliefs and some of its scriptures, or holy writings, with Judaism. There are major differences, however, between the Christian and Jewish faiths. Unlike the Jews, Christians believe that a Jew named Jesus, who was born about 2,000 years ago, was the Christ, or Son of God. Over 1,833,000,000 people now follow Christianity – more than any other world faith. There are many different churches, each with slightly different ways of worship. The three main Christian groups are Orthodox (based in Greece and Eastern Europe), and Roman Catholic and Protestant, both of which have a worldwide following. There are also communities of Coptic Christians in Egypt and Ethiopia. Festivals play a very important part in the Christian year. The holiest ones are Christmas and Easter, but there are also saints' days and many local festivals and thanksgivings. How the festivals are celebrated varies greatly from one part of the world to another. At Lalibela in Ethiopia, white-robed monks welcome Christmas Day with trumpets. In Italy and Spain there are splendid processions through the streets during Holy Week.

▽ ST NICHOLAS
St Nicholas, the patron saint of children, rides a white horse through Amsterdam's streets on 5 December, dressed as a bishop. His Dutch name is Sinterklaas.

◁ CORPUS CHRISTI

Masks, headdresses and brilliantly coloured shawls are worn in the Andes mountains of South America during Corpus Christi. This Roman Catholic festival in June celebrates the Eucharist (the bread and wine used at Holy Communion to represent the body of Christ).

Christianity was brought to South America nearly 500 years ago by Spanish invaders. Although they adopted the Christian faith, many Native Americans kept their own traditions and costumes.

HOLY WEEK

'Semana Santa' is the name given to Holy Week in Spain. Platforms called 'pasos', carrying statues of Jesus and the Virgin Mary, are paraded through the streets.

▷ WELL DRESSING

In Derbyshire, England, wells and springs are decorated with pictures beautifully made out of flowers. Each 'well dressing' honours the patron saint of the village church.

▽ MAIN AREAS OF CHRISTIAN FAITH

Christianity started in south-west Asia, but later spread to Europe and all the other continents. Today it covers the areas shown in red. Its holy cities include Jerusalem and Rome. Christians believe that Jesus was born in a stable in Bethlehem, near Jerusalem.

▽ CELEBRATING CHRISTMAS

Christmas is when Christians celebrate the birth of Jesus. They worship in church and sing carols. Families give each other presents.

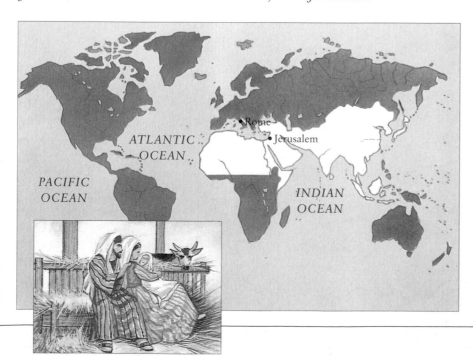

ATLANTIC OCEAN

PACIFIC OCEAN

Rome

Jerusalem

INDIAN OCEAN

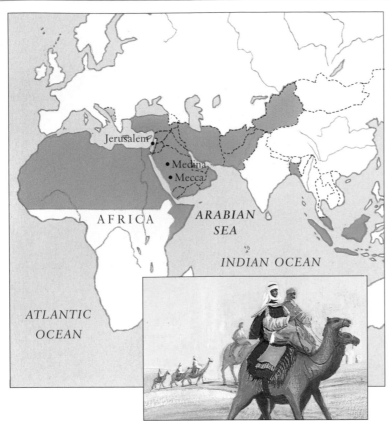

FESTIVALS OF ISLAM

'There is no God but Allah, and Mohammed is the messenger of Allah.' This belief is the heart of Islam. Muslims believe that the words of God were given to Mohammed, who lived between AD 571 and 632, and are written down in the Qu'ran, the holy scriptures of Islam. Muslims honour some of the same holy men as Jews and Christians. Today there are over 1,300,000,000 Muslims in the world. There are two main groups, Sunni and Shi'ite. Muslims pray five times a day facing Mecca, Mohammed's birthplace. Their festivals include fasting, feast days and pilgrimages.

△ AREAS OF ISLAMIC FAITH

Islam started in the deserts of Arabia, but soon spread into large areas of north and east Africa and eastwards into India, China and south-east Asia. Later the Turks brought Islam to south-eastern Europe. Islam's holy cities include Mecca, Medina and Jerusalem. Throughout history pilgrims, like the camel-riders here, have traced the journey of Mohammed from Mecca to the city of Medina. In Medina, Mohammed first established the religion of Islam.

▷ SACRED JOURNEY

Pilgrimage is a sacred duty for Muslims, who try to make the 'Hajj', or pilgrimage to Mecca, at least once in their lifetime. Dressed in white (to show that they are equal in the sight of God), they visit the Grand Mosque and pass seven times around the 'Ka'aba', a chamber with a holy black stone in one corner. Mohammed said that this stone had been given to Abraham by the angel Gabriel.

MAKE A CARD FOR EID UL-FITR

At Eid ul-Fitr you can send a greetings card to your friends. Islamic designs do not include people or animals. They are made up of beautiful swirling patterns, colours and lines.

You will need: a soft pencil, tracing paper, coloured pencil, stiff coloured paper, card, scissors, glue and silver sparkle.

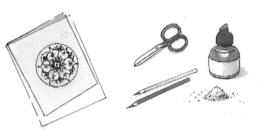

1. Look in your diary to find out the date of Eid ul-Fitr – it changes each year. Trace the pattern shown on this page onto tracing paper, scribble over the back of your tracing paper with a soft pencil and then transfer the tracing onto a sheet of stiff paper.

2. Stick on the sparkle. Cut out the picture carefully and paste it onto a folded piece of card.

3. With the coloured pencil, write your greeting inside.

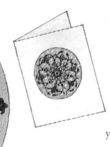

△ EID UL-FITR
Horsemen in traditional robes take part in a splendid procession in Niger, Africa. The end of Ramadan, the ninth month in the Muslim year, is marked by the Islamic festival of Eid ul-Fitr. In the lands to the south of the Sahara Desert, Muslims hold a Sallah, a grand festival.

▷ RAMADAN
This Muslim family is celebrating the end of Ramadan with a special meal in the home. Ramadan is a time of fasting. During this month, Muslims may not eat food during the hours of daylight. Ramadan is an important month for Muslims, for it was during Ramadan that the Qu'ran was first revealed to the prophet Mohammed.

Hindu Festivals

Spectacular festivals and ceremonies play an important part in the Hindu religion. Some of them date back over 4,000 years. Hindus believe that all living things have eternal souls. One person, therefore, leads many lives, and during each life must learn how to understand God.

Hindus believe in one God called Brahma, the great spirit. But this single spirit appears in many different forms, which are worshipped as gods and goddesses. Each is honoured with his or her own special festival. Many Hindus go on pilgrimage. They travel to the River Ganges and other holy sites. Hindus bathe in the Ganges at a town called Varanasi. They believe that this will release their souls from the endless cycle of birth and death.

△ DURGA
The Hindu goddess Durga has 1,000 names. She is honoured each autumn by a ten-day autumn festival, known as Durga Puja or Dussehra. Sacred flames drive away evil, to make worshippers pure.

▷ RAVANA
A huge model of Ravana, the demon king, is burnt on the last day of the Dussehra festival. Ancient poems tell how Ravana was killed by Rama, a form of the great god Vishnu. Ravana had carried off Rama's faithful wife, Sita.

△ HOLI
During the springtime festival of Holi, Hindus in India and Nepal like to play tricks. They run through the streets where they live and throw buckets of coloured water over each other. Soon everybody is stained with dye.

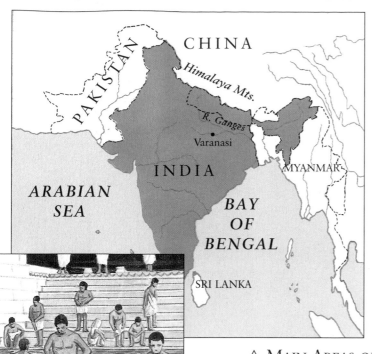

△ MAIN AREAS OF HINDU FAITH

Hinduism first grew up in India, and most of the world's 730 million Hindus still live there today. Many of their festivals are held at famous temples and at holy places such as the town of Varanasi. Hindu festivals may also be seen wherever Indian people have settled around the world.

△ ELEPHANT-HEADED GOD

During the Ganesh Chaturthi festival, a giant statue of Ganesh, the god of wisdom, is carried to the sea near the Indian city of Bombay. Ganesh is said to be the son of the Hindu gods Shiva and Parvati. Legends tell how Shiva cut off Ganesh's head, but replaced it with the head of a wise elephant.

△ DIWALI

Diwali is a beautiful festival held at the start of the Hindu New Year, in October or November. Families light many small lamps in their homes in honour of Lakshmi, the goddess of fortune. Hindus around the world visit friends and relations and give each other cards and presents. They let off fireworks and have special feasts. Business people visit the local temple and pray for good luck in the coming year.

OFFERINGS TO THE GODS

Fruit, vegetables and rice are left at the Taman Pule temple on the island of Bali, in Indonesia. People leave these offerings to the gods in honour of the spirits of their ancestors. This happens at the end of the Galungan festival which celebrates the victory of good over evil. Most Indonesians are Muslims, but on Bali people follow a local form of Hinduism.

SIKH FESTIVALS

Sikhs follow the teachings of ten leaders, or Gurus. The Sikh religion was founded by Guru Nanak, who lived in India about 500 years ago. The main religions at that time were Hinduism and Islam, but Guru Nanak rejected the practices of some of their followers. Over the centuries, the Gurus looked for common ground to bring the two religions together, while establishing a different way of thinking for the Sikh religion.

Sikh men wear the five 'Ks': Kes (long hair, wound under a turban), Kangha (a comb), Kirpan (a sword), Kachh (short trousers) and Kara (a steel bracelet). A Sikh temple, or Gurdwara, is where the holy scriptures, the Guru Granth Sahib, are read. It is also a social centre where people may meet to eat and talk.

Sikhs celebrate religious festivals with music, flowers, flags, processions and readings from the scriptures. Many festivals honour the ten Gurus. Special celebrations are held on the birthdays of Guru Nanak and of Guru Gobind Singh, the founder of the Sikh Brotherhood, or Khalsa. The deaths of Guru Arjan and Guru Tegh Bahadur are also honoured.

Some Sikh festivals are held at the same time as Hindu festivals. At Holi, the Sikh spring festival of Hola Mohalla is celebrated with sporting competitions. At Diwali, Sikhs commemorate the release of Guru Hargobind from prison. Baisakhi, a harvest festival, commemorates Sikhs killed by British troops in the holy city of Amritsar in 1919.

△ FLOWER GARLANDS
A Sikh sells garlands of flowers to wear at a religious festival. Indians of all faiths may wear flowers at festivals, weddings and other special occasions.

HONOURING MARTYRS

Young Sikhs play the bagpipes in a procession in memory of Guru Tegh Bahadur, who was imprisoned by the Emperor Aurangzeb and killed in 1675. He is honoured as a martyr – someone who dies for their religious beliefs.

THE GOLDEN TEMPLE

For the great festivals, many Sikh pilgrims visit the centre of their faith, the Golden Temple at Amritsar. They listen to readings from the holy scriptures. Amritsar is in the Punjab region of north-western India. The city was founded in 1577 by the fourth Guru, Ram Das, the 'servant of God'. The gilded domes of his Golden Temple rise above marble walkways and the still waters of the 'Pool of Immortality'. Pilgrims bathe in the pool before entering the Temple.

▷ MAIN AREAS OF SIKH FAITH

About 18 million people follow the Sikh faith. It is centred in north-western India, around the shrine at Amritsar, but has followers wherever Indians have settled in the world, from East Africa to Canada. Sikhs living overseas worship on whichever day of the week is a holiday locally. The Sikh flag is flown from many Gurdwaras. The Khanda emblem includes a sword, two daggers and a bracelet.

◁ SIKH SCRIPTURES

The Sikh holy scriptures, the Guru Granth Sahib or Adi Granth, are carried in procession at a festival held to open a new Gurdwara in Kenya, Africa. The scriptures play an important part in the life of every Sikh. They are the first words a baby hears on being born, and are at the centre of every Sikh wedding ceremony. Each copy of the scriptures has its own special room and must be treated with great respect.

BUDDHIST FESTIVALS

Buddhists follow the teachings of Siddhartha Gautama, who was born in Nepal in about 563 BC. He was a prince who gave up all his wealth to live a simple life. He realised great truths about the way we live and became known as 'Buddha', the 'Enlightened One'. The Buddha taught that selfishness and personal desire were the causes of human suffering. Buddhists therefore try to lead good lives by not causing suffering to others. They actively try to put others first.

Buddhist monks carried the faith throughout Asia. In many lands Buddhism became mixed with local traditions, and Buddhist festivals still vary greatly from one country to another. Tibetan Buddhists commemorate the religious reformer Tsong Khapa, who lived about 600 years ago, by lighting lamps of yak butter in every window. In Japan, children pour tea over a statue of Buddha, recalling a legend which says that it rained tea on the day Buddha was born. In some countries, caged birds are set free on Buddha's birthday (Wesak). Many Buddhists visit monasteries in July, during the festival of Dhammacakka which celebrates Buddha's first teachings.

△ RITUAL SHAVING
In this Burmese ceremony, small boys relive the life of Buddha. First they are dressed in the fine clothes of a prince, then their heads are shaved and they are dressed in monks' robes.

▷ MAIN AREAS OF BUDDHIST FAITH
Buddhism has two divisions – Hinayana (followed in Sri Lanka and south-east Asia) and Mahayana (in north-east Asia). It is the world's fourth largest religion, with 315,000,000 followers. Countries that are mostly Buddhist are shown in dark green; countries that are partly Buddhist are in pale green. The Shwe Dagon Pagoda in Myanmar (Burma), shown here, is a centre of pilgrimage.

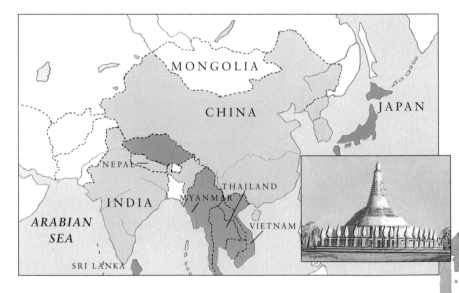

SACRED MUSIC

Buddhist priests called 'lamas' play deep, booming horns during a ceremony at the Ta Gong monastery in Tibet. Before the Tibetan New Year, people clean out their houses and whitewash the walls, to chase away any bad memories. When the New Year festival arrives, monks chant, play the horns and dance. There are processions, sporting contests and feasting.

▷ DEMON MASK

This monk has put on the terrifying mask of a demon decorated with skulls, for the dances which bring in the Tibetan New Year. The dancers aim to scare away evil spirits. Whereas Buddha taught a very simple personal faith, in some parts of the world the religion came to include complicated beliefs in gods, spirits and a large number of saints.

△ BUDDHA'S BIRTHDAY

The birthday of Buddha is honoured by a priest at the Zojoji temple in Japan. The festival, which also commemorates Buddha's death in 483 BC, is celebrated in April by Buddhists everywhere but in many different ways. They may visit a temple or make gifts to monasteries.

▽ SACRED TOOTH OF BUDDHA

The 'Perahera' (great procession) in the town of Kandy, Sri Lanka, is held at full moon in the summer month of Esala. Like the followers of other religions, Buddhists on Sri Lanka honour holy relics, or remains. This torchlight procession honours the Buddha's Sacred Tooth, kept in a shrine at the Dalada Maligawa temple. The Esala Perahera has dancing, music and elephants.

OTHER BELIEFS, OTHER CEREMONIES

The world has as many religions as it does peoples, and some of them are very ancient. Many African peoples believe in a spirit world, in gods of nature and in honouring ancestors. Some hold beautiful festivals with dancing and masks. The Aboriginal peoples of Australia recall a 'dreamtime', when the spirits of creation were loosed upon the Earth. They hold certain animals and places to be sacred.

The Jains of India will harm no living thing, even insects. The Parsees of India follow the teachings of the Persian prophet Zoroaster, who lived over 2,500 years ago. Zoroaster saw life as a struggle between the god of goodness and light and the god of violence and death. In China, Buddhism is mixed with the beliefs of Taoism and Confucianism, which teaches social harmony and respect for one's ancestors. In Japan, Buddhism exists side by side with the Shinto religion, which teaches purity and the worship of the forces of nature.

All these religions have their own ceremonies, rituals and festivals. Many of them are similar. It seems that all people love dance, music, fire and light, chanting and wearing masks or paint or robes. Some people believe that all religious festivals and ceremonies are different paths to the same 'truth'. And even people who are atheists, not believing in any god at all, enjoy festivals and fun.

△ CORROBOREE
Aboriginal Australians hold sacred festivals called corroborees. Many of their dances are based on tales of animal spirits. Music is played on the didgeridoo, a long pipe.

▷ MEXICAN VOLADORS
Aztec warriors of ancient Mexico used to 'fly' at one religious festival. Dressed like birds, they jumped off the top of a high pole. They were tied to the pole by ropes, so they whirled around and around through the air before landing. Their flight was meant to be like that of the Sun across the sky. This 'Volador' ceremony may still be seen in Mexico today.

▽ WORSHIP OF THE SUN
Stonehenge, a circle of huge stones, was built in England about 3,500 years ago. Nobody knows what religious ceremonies took place there. Every Midsummmer's Eve, worshippers calling themselves 'Druids' gather at the stones to welcome the Sun. They are not the same as the historical Druids, who were ancient Celtic priests.

A Code of Honour

At this ceremony at the Chongmyo shrine in South Korea, Confucian priests honour the royal ancestors of the Yi family, who ruled Korea until 1910. Confucius was a Chinese thinker who lived 2,500 years ago. He believed in ritual and social harmony, and taught that these values should decide the way we behave. Children should honour their parents, parents should honour ancestors, and everyone should honour their ruler.

▽ Prayers for World Unity

At this Baha'i festival in Fiji, people pray for world unity. The Baha'i faith started up in Iran in the last century. Baha'is believe that all the great world scriptures are sacred, and that all religions worship the same God, who cannot be known. About 4,500,000 people around the world now follow the Baha'i faith.

CALENDAR OF FESTIVALS

Many festivals, such as national holidays, birthday celebrations and anniversaries, take place on the same date each year. But sometimes the birthdays of kings and queens do not fall on a convenient day, so they have two birthdays – a real one and an 'official' one! Many religious festivals are very ancient and are based on the appearance of the moon or on religious calendars. That is why festivals such as Easter, Eid ul-Fitr and the Chinese New Year all take place on a different date each year.

▷ ESALA PERAHERA
Procession of elephants, Sri Lanka, July-August

△ ST LUCY'S DAY
Festival of light, Sweden, 13 December

JANUARY
6   Twelfth Night or Epiphany, Christian feast of the Three Kings
6-7   Orthodox Christian feast of Christmas
15/16   Martin Luther King Day, USA
25   Burns Night, Scotland
26   Republic Day, India
      Australia Day

JANUARY-FEBRUARY
Chinese spring festival (New Year)
Tet (Vietnamese New Year)

FEBRUARY
Argungu fishing festival, Nigeria
2   Groundhog Day, USA
6   Waitangi Day, New Zealand
11   National Accession Day, Japan
14   St Valentine's Day, for those in love
22   Washington's Birthday, USA

FEBRUARY-MARCH
Shrove Tuesday (Mardi Gras, Fastnacht, Pancake Day)
Carnival
Jewish festival of Purim
Hindu festival of Mahashivaratri

MARCH
1   St David's Day (National Day of Wales)
3   Japanese doll festival (Hina-Matsuri)
6   National Day, Ghana
8   International Women's Day
17   St Patrick's Day (National Day of Ireland)
20   Spring festival, Japan
23   National Day, Pakistan
25   National Day, Greece

MARCH-APRIL
Moomba festival, Melbourne, Australia
Protestant and Catholic Christians celebrate Easter
Jewish festival of Pesach (Passover)
Hindu festival of Holi, Sikh Holi Mohalla
Hindu festival of Rama Naumi
Chinese festival of remembrance, Qing Ming
Mother's Day, UK

APRIL
1   All Fools' Day
8   Buddha's birthday celebrated in Japan
13   Sikh festival of Baisakhi
23   St George's Day (National Day, England)
      Turkish children's festival
25   Anzac Day, Australia and New Zealand
30   National Day, Netherlands

APRIL-MAY
Feria in Seville, Spain
Orthodox Christians celebrate Easter

MAY
Cheung Chau bun festival, Hong Kong
Mother's Day (USA)
1   May Day (spring festival)
      International Workers' Day
5   Boy's Day, Japan
17   National Day, Norway

MAY-JUNE
Jewish festival of Shavuot
Christian festival of Pentecost (Whitsun)
Buddhist festival of Wesak (Buddha's birthday)
Sikhs commemorate Guru Arjan

JUNE
Dragon Boat festival, China
Trooping the Colour, London
Christian festival of Corpus Christi
Father's Day
2   Republic Day, Italy
6   National Day, Sweden
12   Russian Independence Day
23   Midsummer's Eve
24   Festival of St John the Baptist (Quebec)

JULY
Buddhist festival of Dhammacakka
1   National Day, Canada
4   US Independence Day
9   National Day, Argentina
14   Bastille Day (French National Day)
18   National Day, Spain
21   National Day, Belgium
22   National Day, Poland

◁ GUY FAWKES' DAY
Bonfire night, Great Britain, 5 November

▷ CORONATIONS AND STATE CEREMONIES
Asante ruler, Ghana

▷ CHINESE NEW YEAR
China and Chinese communities, January-February

▷ DUSSEHRA
Hindu festival,
October

▷ RAMADAN
Muslims mark the end
of Ramadan
with a
special
meal

JULY-AUGUST
Esala Perahera, Sri Lanka
O-Bon (family remembrance day), Japan

AUGUST
Hindu family festival of Raksha Bandhan
Notting Hill carnival, London
Edinburgh Arts festival, Scotland
National Eisteddfod of Wales
1   National Day, Switzerland
6   National Day, Bolivia
17   National Day, Indonesia

AUGUST-SEPTEMBER
Hindu festival of Janmashtami

SEPTEMBER
Chinese Moon Festival
7   National Day, Brazil
16   National Day, Mexico
18   National Day, Chile
30   National Day, Botswana

SEPTEMBER-OCTOBER
Jewish New Year (Rosh Hashanah)
Jewish Day of Atonement (Yom Kippur)
Jewish festival of Succot

OCTOBER
Hindu festival of Dussehra (Durga Puja)
1   National Day, China
9   National Day, Uganda
12   Columbus Day
24   United Nations' Day
     National Day, Zambia
26   National Day, Austria
31   Halloween

OCTOBER-NOVEMBER
Hindus and Sikhs celebrate Diwali
Sikhs celebrate Guru Nanak's birthday

NOVEMBER
Thanksgiving Day, USA
1   Christian festival of All Saints
2   Mahayana Buddhists celebrate
     Bodhi Day

     Mexican Day of the Dead (All Souls)
5   Guy Fawkes Day, Great Britain
7   Russians commemorate October
     Revolution of 1917
     Armistice Day, First World War
30   St Andrew's Day (National Day,
     Scotland)

DECEMBER
Jewish festival of Hanukkah
Chinese winter festival
Kwanzaa (African-American festival)
5   Festival of St Nicholas Netherlands
     National Day, Finland
9   National Day, Tanzania
12   National Day, Kenya
13   St Lucy's Day (Swedish festival)
24   Catholic/Protestant Christmas Eve
25   Catholic/Protestant Christians celebrate
     Christmas
26   Feast of St Stephen, Boxing Day
     (England)
31   New Year's Eve, Hogmanay

DECEMBER-JANUARY
Sikhs celebrate birthday of Guru Gobind
   Singh
Sikhs honour the martyrdom of Guru Tegh
   Bahadur

MOVABLE ISLAMIC FESTIVALS

Hijrah New Year
Ashura'
Birthday of Prophet Mohammed
Lailat ul-Isra wal Mi'raj
Lailat ul-Bara'h
Ramadan
Lailat ul-Qadr
Eid ul-Fitr
Arafat
Eid ul-Adha

△ PURIM
Jewish festival,
February-March

△ HALLOWEEN
USA, parts of British Isles, English-
speaking communities, 31 October

△ OLYMPIC GAMES
Worldwide
Every four years

◁ FISHING FESTIVAL
Argungu, Nigeria
February

▷ ST NICHOLAS'
DAY
Sinterklaas,
Netherlands,
5 December

GLOSSARY

ANNIVERSARY
Any celebration which marks the date of a past event, such as a wedding or a famous victory.

CARNIVAL
A week of celebrations traditionally held in the week before the Christian fast of Lent – the word literally means 'stop eating meat'. Carnival includes wild celebrations, fancy dress, dancing and public processions. The word is also used to describe any similar festival. In southern Germany, carnival is called Fasching.

CAROL
Any traditional song of joy – especially a Christmas hymn.

CELEBRATE
To take part in a festival, a ceremony or a commemoration, or to enjoy oneself on a happy occasion.

CELTIC FESTIVALS
Any of the seasonal festivals (Imbole, Beltain etc.) held by the Celtic peoples of Europe before they became Christians about 1,600 years ago.

CEREMONY
Any special action which has to take place at an important religious or public event.

COMMEMORATION
An event at which people gather to remember a particular historical event or person.

CORONATION
The placing of a crown on the head of a king, queen or emperor to mark the start of their rule. Coronations are normally marked by grand public celebrations.

CORPUS CHRISTI
A Christian festival celebrating the body of Christ, which is symbolised by bread at the service of Holy Communion.

CORROBOREE
An Aboriginal Australian gathering for sacred dance or story-telling.

DHAMMACAKKA
A festival celebrating the first sermon preached by the Buddha.

DIWALI
A Hindu festival of light held in the autumn.

DURGA PUJA
Dussehra, autumn festival of the Hindu mother goddess.

EMBLEM
A flower or other item worn as a kind of badge on a national day. A shamrock is worn on St Patrick's Day, a daffodil or leek is worn on St David's Day.

EXPO
Short for Exposition (Exhibition), an 'Expo' is a world fair in which each country puts on exhibitions about its arts, sciences or way of life.

FAIR
An amusement show with stalls and rides; a market for selling farm animals or produce; a yearly trade gathering or international exhibition.

FAST
A period when people eat nothing or very little, for religious reasons. Ramadan is an Islamic fast. Lent is a Christian one.

GANESH CHATURTHI
A festival honouring the Hindu god Ganesh.

GURU
An Indian religious teacher. The Sikhs honour ten gurus as founders of their faith.

HANUKKAH
A Jewish festival of lights.

HARVEST FESTIVAL
Any festival held to give thanks for the harvesting of crops and for the food which keeps us alive.

HOLI
A Hindu spring festival marked by processions and the throwing of coloured water.

HOLIDAY
Originally a 'holy day'. The word now means any period which people may take off work or school.

INTI RAYMI
An Inca festival of the Sun held at Cuzco, Peru.

KWANZAA
A harvest thanksgiving celebrated by African-Americans.

MARDI GRAS
Shrove Tuesday, the day before the Christian period of Lent. 'Mardi Gras' is French for 'Fat Tuesday', the day on which foods were used up before fasting began.

MAYPOLE
A tall wooden pole decorated with ribbons or flowers for May Day.

MILLENIUM
A period of 1,000 years, usually celebrated with a special festival.

MUMMERS
In the Middle Ages, revellers who dressed up in fancy dress and sang or acted during Christmas and other festivals.

NATIONAL DAY
A day set aside as a holiday to honour the nation.

NEW YEAR'S DAY
The start of a new calendar, which different peoples celebrate at different times. The Scottish New Year's Eve is called Hogmanay. The Vietnamese New Year is called Tet.

OLYMPIC GAMES
The world's most important international sports event started thousands of years ago as a religious festival held at Olympia, in ancient Greece.

PATRON SAINT
A saint is a person who Christians believe has led a very holy life. Patron saints are thought to look after a particular group of people, a profession or a country. Every saint has his or her own festival or holy day each year.

PERAHERA
One of the great processions held in Sri Lanka.

PESACH
Passover, a Jewish spring festival celebrated with a special meal.

PILGRIMAGE
A journey or procession to a holy place. Some of the world's greatest religious festivals, such as the Islamic Hajj, are pilgrimages.

PURIM
A Jewish spring festival.

PROCESSION
Walking in a line, for a parade, a ceremony or a religious display.

RAMADAN
The month of fasting held by Muslims. It is ended by the festival of Eid ul-Fitr.

RAKSHA BANDHAN
A Hindu festival for brothers and sisters.

RELIC
The remains of a saint or other holy person, believed to be sacred.

RITUAL
A formal act which is part of a religious ceremony, such as the lighting of a flame.

SATURNALIA
A Roman winter festival which included wild celebrations and the exchange of gifts. Masters waited on their servants at table. Some Christmas and Carnival customs date back to Saturnalia.

SHAVUOT
Pentecost, a Jewish festival celebrating the Law of Moses.

SHRINE
A holy place visited by pilgrims, or a casket or chamber containing holy objects.

SUCCOT
A festival commemorating the days spent by the Jews in the desert in ancient times.

SYMBOL
An object, custom or act which stands for an idea or a belief.

WELL DRESSING
The decoration of wells with holy pictures made of flowers – a way of celebrating Christian saints' days in the English county of Derbyshire.

WESAK
A celebration of the Buddha's birth, enlightenment and death.

YOM KIPPUR
A day of fasting and repentance for Jewish people.

INDEX